For Mum
Now my guiding light in Spirit

HARK
PUBLICATIONS

Published by HARK Publications

© Amanda Seyderhelm 2012
© Illustrations by Ann Scott

Amanda Seyderhelm asserts the moral right to be identified as the
author of this work.

ISBN 978-0-9572146-1-3

British Library Cataloguing-in-Publication Data
A catalogue record for this book is available from the British Library.

10% of proceeds are donated to www.treetopshospice.org.uk

www.helpingchildrensmileagain.com

Isaac hadn't picked up his knitting needles for weeks. He was heartbroken when his best friend Freddie died. No-one explained where Freddie had gone. Isaac couldn't help but wonder if he had said something to upset Freddie...

Isaac and Freddie had bonded over wool. Out of school hours they knitted magic jumpers for their friends in Isacc's garden shed. Tucked inside each jumper was an inspirational message from them. When the Magic Jumpers were worn they made people feel more confident and happy, and had a way of knitting together the gaps in peoples' lives. Really it was Isaac and Freddie's friendship that could be felt in every stitch. People felt special when they wore a Magic Jumper.

4

Together they could achieve anything!

Without Freddie, Isaac felt his heart freezing over. Worse still, he stopped seeing the world in vivid colour. He lost his desire to knit, and even his red jumper suddenly turned grey. His little house felt so cold that the walls literally froze. Monty and Bill decided to take matters into their own hands and call Jenny, Isaac's neighbour.

Jenny was happy to help. She tried to comfort Isaac with her homemade cookies, but Isaac despaired of ever feeling normal again. He just wanted someone to tell him where Freddie was, and how he could see colours again. He had moments of fun with Jenny but then he felt sad.

"Do you think Freddie can knit where he is?" asked Isaac
"Probably in psychadelic purple", replied Jenny. "I think he
sits in the stars at night and watches us."
Bill and Monty agreed.

Isaac moped about on his window ledge. "I hope Freddie is wearing his jumper"
said Isaac. "I haven't felt like knitting stripes or circles for weeks now.
It's no fun without Freddie."

Jenny tried to make Isaac smile again by dancing. She and Rob staged a performance for Isaac wearing their favourite Magic Jumpers.

Jenny knew that Isaac had a secret sweet tooth so she baked him his favourite biscuits with red icing, picked wild red poppies from her garden, and painted beautiful paintings to inspire him back to colour.

Nothing cheered Isaac up. His teeth started to chatter. He couldn't move his hands.
He couldn't eat. No knitting for him. His whole world felt cold.

Jenny hoped for a miracle. She closed her eyes, and folded her hands together, and imagined Isaac's life being colourful again.

One day, Isaac was sitting on his window ledge dozing when Freddie floated by holding an umbrella. Freddie was smiling at Isaac. Around him there was an orange glow. Isaac could feel the warmth from the glow.

Jenny gasped as she saw Freddie hanging from his umbrella.   They both waved at
Freddie. The room was filled with an incredible warmth, and for a moment they both
danced with excitement.

When they looked back Freddie had gone but they felt warmer than
they had done in ages.

Jenny heard a dripping noise. "Look Isaac, the ice is melting!" Jenny said.

They touched the walls. Indeed the ice was melting!

Jenny looked at Isaac. He was no longer grey and frozen, and the colour was coming back to his jumper! Isaac's despair suddenly lifted.
"I know where Freddie is, and I know he's safe. He will always look out for me even though I can't see him. Whenever I want to talk to him I can just close my eyes and imagine him there with me" said Isaac.

"Look" shouted Jenny.
Isaac looked in the mirror. His Magic Jumper had returned to its rosy red colour.
The house was no longer grey nor icy, and neither was Isacc's heart.
Those knitting needles beckoned ...

Questions for an adult to ask a bereaved child.

Here are some questions to ask a bereaved child that will help them to heal their grief process:

- What do you imagine Isaac knitted? Can you draw it?

- If you knitted a Magic Jumper what special message would you tuck inside it?

- If you could knit a jumper for someone you know who has died, what colours would you use? Can you draw your jumper? What special messa ge would you put in it for them?

- Jenny thought Freddie was in the stars looking down. What do you believe might happen to people when they die?

- Jenny kept trying to cheer Isaac up and not being able to How would this feel? Do you sometimes feel like that?

- What do you like to do to cheer yourself up when you feel sad?

- Jenny was a good friend to Isaac. Do you have a good friend, or someone in your family, who is there for you when you feel sad?

Amanda Seyderhelm is an author and PTUK
Certified Therapeutic Play Practitioner.

Amanda uses her play therapy tool kit (sandtray,
art, clay, music, drama, dance and movement,
puppets, masks, storytelling and creative
visualisation) to help children smile again,
develop self-esteem and reach their full potential.

Amanda lives in Rutland with her husband Peter.

www.helpingchildrensmileagain.com

HARK
PUBLICATIONS

Lightning Source UK Ltd.
Milton Keynes UK
UKRC01n1927051116
286955UK00002B/2